CASTLES

Created by Gallimard Jeunesse,
Claude Delafosse and C. & D. Millet
Illustrated by C. & D. Millet

A FIRST DISCOVERY BOOK

Cartwheel
·B·O·O·K·S·™

SCHOLASTIC INC.
New York   Toronto   London   Auckland   Sydney

Hundreds of years ago,
in the Middle Ages,
the nobles of Europe
lived in large, well-protected castles.

The castles were fortresses
surrounded by high stone walls.

When visitors wished to enter the castle,
servants had to lower a drawbridge . . .

and raise a heavy iron gate
called a portcullis.

Inside the
castle walls,
the people were safe
from their enemies.

It was like a small town.
The poultry yard was where
the animals were kept.

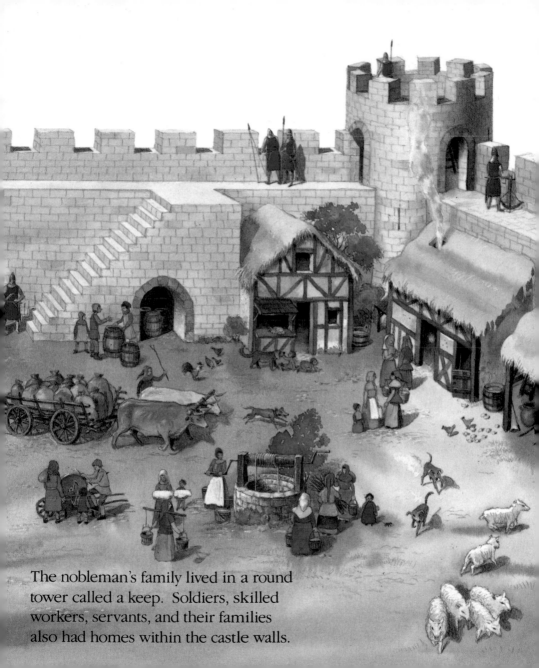

The nobleman's family lived in a round
tower called a keep. Soldiers, skilled
workers, servants, and their families
also had homes within the castle walls.

There was no electricity, running water,
or heat. On cold nights the
whole family might . . .

The bedrooms were decorated with beautiful tapestries.

sleep in one bed to keep warm!

The gigantic stone ovens, fiery spits,
and boiling cauldrons
were going night and day!

The kitchen was
a busy place!

The servants prepared enough
fish, meat, bread, and cheese
for everyone in the castle.
The people ate few vegetables.

Lords and ladies
from
neighboring
castles . . .

Jugglers and jesters
made everyone laugh.

came to
feasts in
the great
hall.

But the most popular performers
were the trained bears.

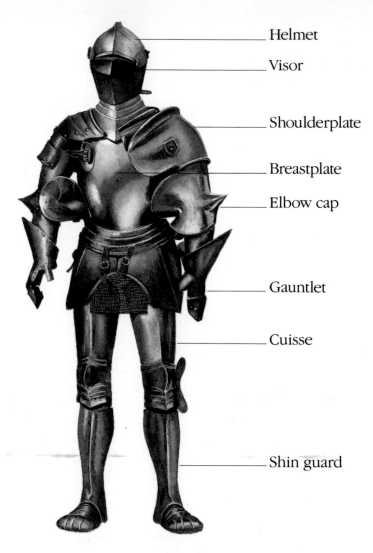

Helmet

Visor

Shoulderplate

Breastplate

Elbow cap

Gauntlet

Cuisse

Shin guard

Knights were the soldiers of their day.
They wore heavy armor made of iron.

A knight's metal armor was lined with soft quilting
to protect his skin. The armor was so heavy,
a knight needed help to mount his horse!

Knights often entertained the nobles with fighting contests called jousting tournaments.

The horses were protected from the swords and lances by their own armor.

Sometimes war broke out between the nobles!

The enemy soldiers
climbed great
scaling ladders
to leap over
the castle wall!

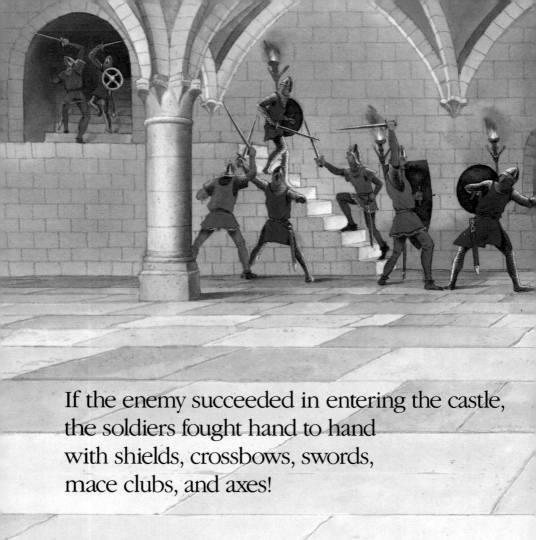

If the enemy succeeded in entering the castle,
the soldiers fought hand to hand
with shields, crossbows, swords,
mace clubs, and axes!

Some unlucky soldiers
landed in the cold, dark
dungeon below the floor.

Today, many castles
are left in ruins.

But a few still exist.
You can see suits of armor,
weapons, and tapestries in museums.
And you can read exciting books
about the days of lords, ladies, and knights
in shining armor!

Titles in the series of *First Discovery Books*:

Airplanes	**The Earth and Sky**
and Flying Machines	**The Egg**
Bears	**Flowers**
Birds	**Fruit**
Castles	**The Ladybug**
Cats	**and Other Insects**
Colors	**The Tree**
Dinosaurs	**Weather**

Library of Congress Cataloging-in-Publication Data available.
Originally published in France in 1990 by Editions Gallimard.

ISBN 0-590-46377-2
Copyright © 1990 by Editions Gallimard.
This edition English translation by Jennifer Riggs.
This edition American text by Nancy Krulik.
All rights reserved. First published in the U.S.A. in 1993 by Scholastic Inc., by arrangement with Editions Gallimard, 5 rue Sebastien-Bottin, F-75007 Paris, France.
CARTWHEEL BOOKS is a trademark of Scholastic Inc.

12 11 10 9 8 7 6 5 4 3 2   3 4 5 6 7 8/9

Printed in Italy by Editoriale Libraria

First Scholastic printing, June 1993